The List
1225 Evergreen Lane

Gene Natali, Jr. & Matt Kabala

ILLUSTRATED BY MIKE DEAN

ISBN 978-0-9855315-4-6

Illustrations by Mike Dean.
Book design and layout by Hunt Smith Design.

First printing edition, 2019.

The Missing Semester, LLC
467 Troutwood Drive
Pittsburgh, PA 15237

Dedication

To children everywhere, just be brave enough to try.

– Gene and Matt

Molly watched the snow-covered pine trees pass. Sam, her younger brother, slept in the seat beside her. It was a long drive to Grandma and Grandpa's house each Christmas.

When Mom's old red van pulled into the familiar driveway, Molly smiled. 1225 Evergreen Lane.

After helping unpack, Molly and Sam headed to their room. Grandpa followed. "I have a surprise for you in the attic," he whispered. Immediately Sam raced past Molly and scrambled up the attic stairs.

3

In the attic was a fireplace where one log still burned. Near the fireplace was a desk, with a lamp and a large, mysterious-looking brown leather book.

Grandpa walked to the fire, bent down, and added a log. Then he motioned for Molly and Sam to join him in his chair. "Can you keep a secret?" Grandpa asked, as he picked up the book. Molly loved Grandpa's stories, and with a smile she nestled close. It had been a long day, and she closed her eyes. For just a moment.

When Molly reopened her eyes, Grandpa's voice stopped. He was now wearing a soft, bright-red coat with furry white cuffs. "Ho, ho, ho," chuckled Grandpa. *Could it be?* thought Molly.

Grandpa was still holding the mysterious book. "Molly, this book is Santa's..."

Chime Chime Chime

The outline of a small gold door appeared beside the fireplace, interrupting Grandpa.

A tiny elf in a green hat shuffled through the door. The elf stopped, stared at Molly, then at Grandpa,...then again at Molly. "Santa, a real girl? In the North Pole!" With a wink at Molly, Grandpa looked at the elf. "Maddie, this is Molly. She's here to help."

Grandpa picked up where he had left off, "Molly, this book is Santa's *List*. It names every girl and boy in the world. Each year it grows larger, and my sleigh heavier." He peered down at Molly over his eyeglasses and chuckled, "Dancer and Prancer aren't getting any younger." Grandpa looked out the door beyond Maddie, "the reindeer of the North Pole live in the forest around my home. There is one whose help we want, but we need *your* help first."

"I'll do it, Grandpa," she blurted.

"I knew you would, Molly," he said with a smile.

Maddie led the way to the reindeer forest. "Up here," she said, motioning. Molly could see reindeer. They were playing! Laughing, she ran behind Maddie.

In the middle of the clearing she watched a small reindeer help pull a friend out of a snow drift. The small reindeer tugged until her larger friend burst out of the snow pile. When they stood up to rejoin the game, Molly noticed something different about the small reindeer. Her two front legs were white almost up to her knees. "Hurry, Socks," yelled her friend. "You're gonna get tagged."

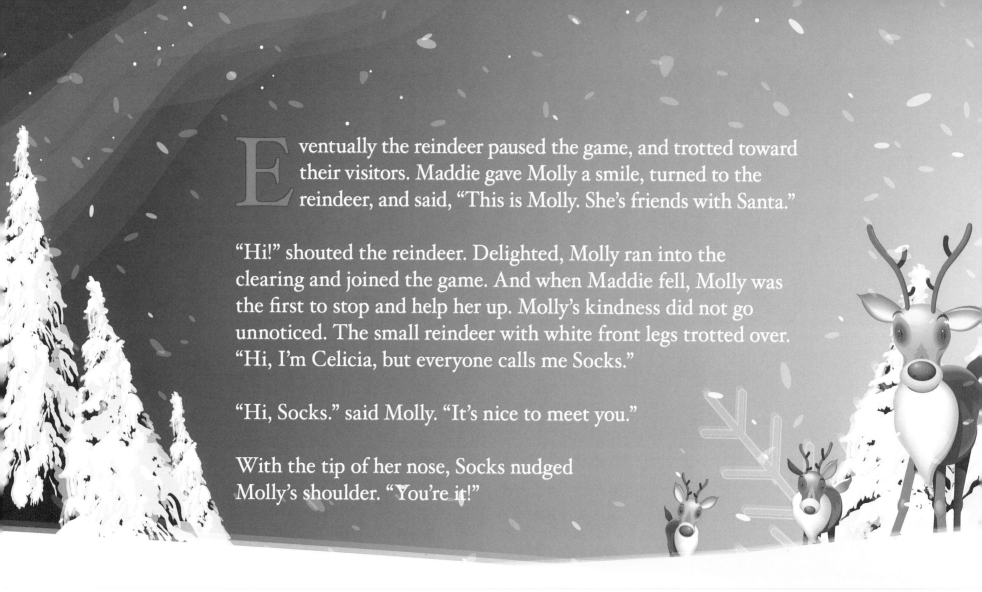

Eventually the reindeer paused the game, and trotted toward their visitors. Maddie gave Molly a smile, turned to the reindeer, and said, "This is Molly. She's friends with Santa."

"Hi!" shouted the reindeer. Delighted, Molly ran into the clearing and joined the game. And when Maddie fell, Molly was the first to stop and help her up. Molly's kindness did not go unnoticed. The small reindeer with white front legs trotted over. "Hi, I'm Celicia, but everyone calls me Socks."

"Hi, Socks." said Molly. "It's nice to meet you."

With the tip of her nose, Socks nudged Molly's shoulder. "You're it!"

13

"MOOOLLLLYYYYYY, IT'S TIME FOR DINNNNNNN-ERRR."

Maddie came running over. "Molly, Santa's calling. We'd better get home." Molly smiled as she watched Maddie turn and head toward Grandpa's house. It was hard to believe that she had spent the afternoon playing with elves and reindeer, and that her grandfather was Santa.

When she looked back toward the clearing, she was startled by a reindeer nose inches from her own. "Bye, Molly," said Socks. "I had fun playing with you today."

The next morning Molly awoke to the smell of candy-cane pancakes, Grandpa's *famous* candy-cane pancakes. While they ate, Grandpa and Maddie told stories about the North Pole: stories of other elves, Santa's workshop, their favorite reindeer, and how many cookies Santa ate.

A knock on the door interrupted Maddie telling Molly that her Grandpa ate *too many* cookies. Grandpa gave Molly a guilty grin and walked to the door.

"Can Molly come out and play?" came a voice from outside. "SOCKS!" shouted Molly, recognizing the voice.

Never straying far from Grandpa's house, Socks led Molly on a grand tour of the North Pole. "Santa's reindeer are the most majestic in the North Pole," Socks explained.

"Mother always hoped that one day I could join Santa's sleigh. That's the dream of every North Pole reindeer." The young reindeer lowered her voice, "Except me. I'm afraid to fly."

"Socks you've shown me what you love. May I show you what I love?" asked Molly. She then began to spin gracefully across the snow. Socks felt an instant joy watching Molly dance, and before she knew it, the small reindeer was dancing alongside.

When Molly slowed to a stop, her head sank. "I love to dance, but I was afraid to try out for the Christmas recital *again* this year." Socks stepped close, and with her nose, gently lifted Molly's head. "You can do it. Just be brave enough to try."

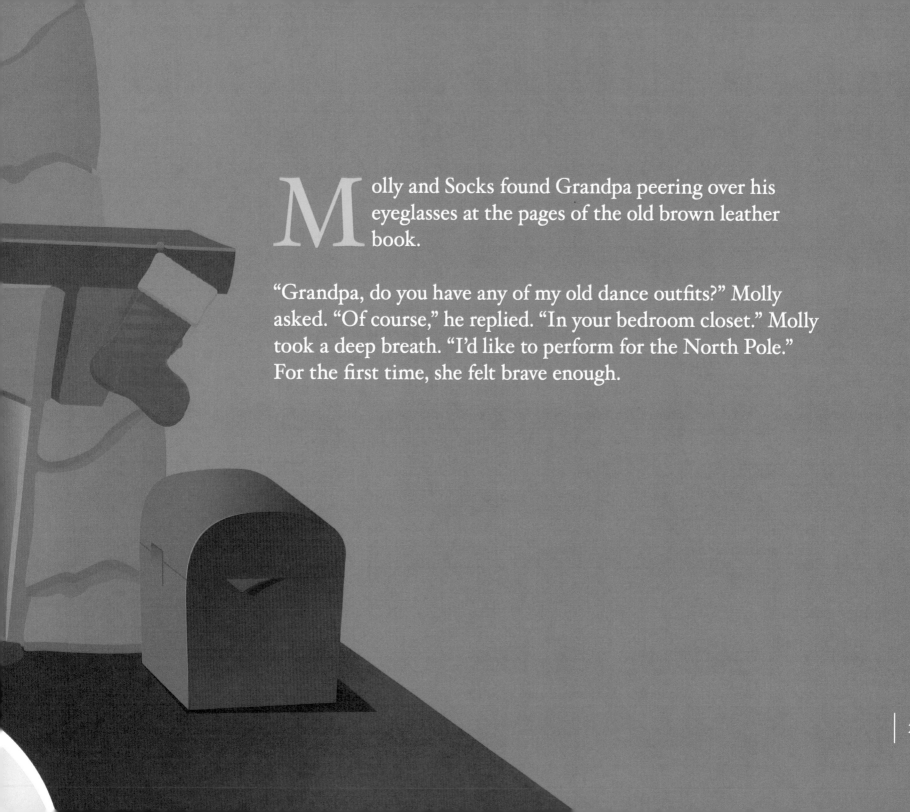

M olly and Socks found Grandpa peering over his eyeglasses at the pages of the old brown leather book.

"Grandpa, do you have any of my old dance outfits?" Molly asked. "Of course," he replied. "In your bedroom closet." Molly took a deep breath. "I'd like to perform for the North Pole." For the first time, she felt brave enough.

After a final leap, Molly took a bow to shouts and applause from the elves, hoof stomps from the reindeer, and loudest of all, a joy-filled "**Ho, Ho, Ho,**" from Grandpa. Molly beamed.

"YOU DID IT, MOLLY!" shouted Socks.

"*WE did it*," said Molly, wrapping her arms tightly around Sock's neck. It was the first real-girl hug that Socks had ever received. Molly then whispered, "Socks, you were right. We can do almost anything if we are brave enough to try...even fly."

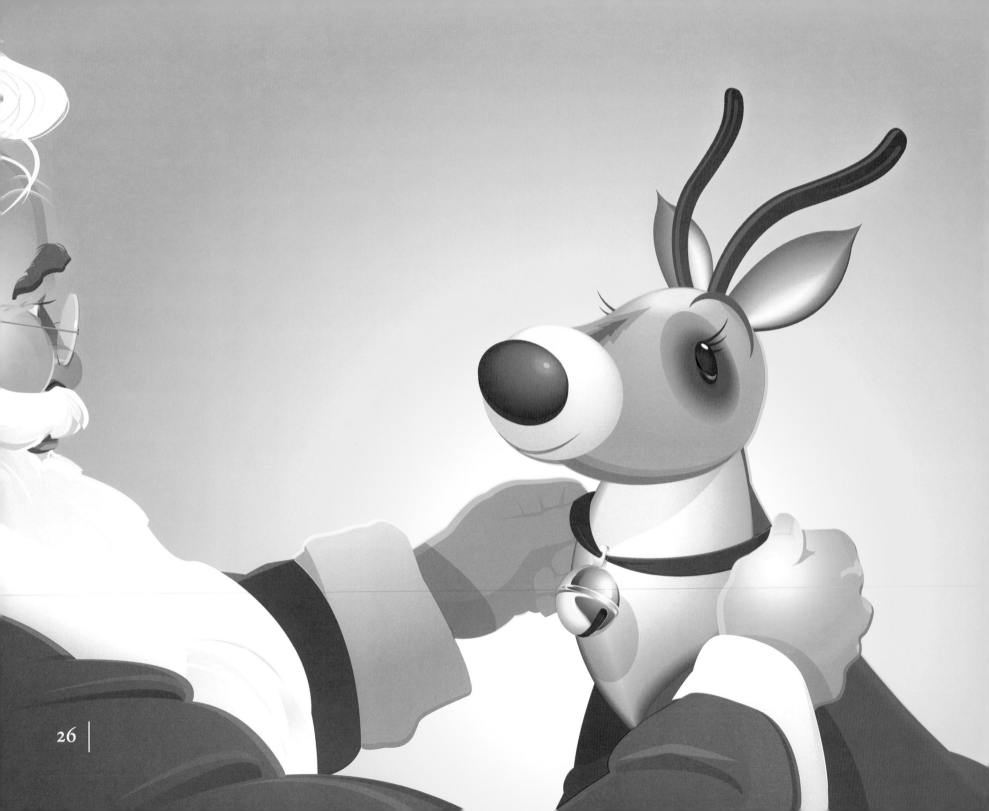

G randpa stepped towards Socks and bent down. "Socks, your love and caring for others shines bright across the North Pole. *There is no greater gift.*"

Grandpa lifted a small bell from the pocket of his red jacket. It was the bell that each of Santa's reindeer wore, filled with North Pole magic that helped them fly on Christmas Eve. Wearing the bell was the greatest honor in the North Pole. "Socks, will you join my sleigh?"

M olly looked around the room. *It was the best Christmas ever.* She was proud of Socks, who looked down at the bell now hanging snugly around her neck. With a smile, Molly moved closer to Grandpa.

It had been a long day, and she closed her eyes. For just a moment.

Molly opened her eyes. She was back in Grandpa's lap, where Sam remained asleep. The old leather-bound book was on the desk, closed. *Where was Socks? Maddie? Was it real?*

Grandpa handed Molly an old snow-globe and an envelope. She watched the snow swirl around what looked like Grandpa's house, with reindeer flying above. Helping to lead the sleigh was a small reindeer with white front legs.

Then she opened the envelope. Inside was a letter:

Molly gasped and looked up at Grandpa. His eyes twinkled as he leaned close and whispered,

"Just be brave enough to try. I love you, Molly."

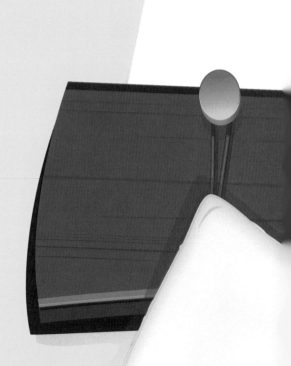